Dear Parent,

In What Is the ... your child will
learn what's on the moon. With the
help of Wise Owl's telescope,
Christopher and his friends get a
bird's-eye view of the moon. Wise Owl
also tells about the astronauts who
have gone to the moon. Get ready to
turn the page—5 . . . 4 . . . 3 . . . 2 . . . 1
. . . blast off!

Sincerely,

Rita D. Gould

Managing Editor

FAMILY FUN

- Look out the window at the moon with your child just before bedtime. Ask your child to draw a picture of the shape of the moon (or the phase of the moon). Repeat the procedure once a week for a month, or until the shape of the moon resembles your child's first drawing. Hang the pictures in a window.

- Play the part of Earth and ask your child to be the moon. Earth stands in the center of the room, and the moon travels in a circle (or rotates) around it.

READ MORE ABOUT IT

- *What Is a Space Shuttle?*
- *What Makes Day and Night?*

This book is a presentation of Weekly Reader
Books. Weekly Reader Books offers book
clubs for children from preschool through high
school. For further information write to:
WEEKLY READER BOOKS, 4343 Equity Drive,
Columbus, Ohio 43228

This edition is published by arrangement
with Checkerboard Press.

Weekly Reader is a federally registered trademark
of Field Publications.

WEEKLY READER BOOKS presents

What Is the Moon?

A **Just Ask**™ Book

Hi, my name is Christopher!

by Chris Arvetis
and Carole Palmer

illustrated by
James Buckley

FIELD PUBLICATIONS
MIDDLETOWN, CT.

The craters are made when
hard things hit the moon.
Some of the craters look
like volcanoes.

The moon has valleys, too. The long narrow ones look like big cracks in the moon.